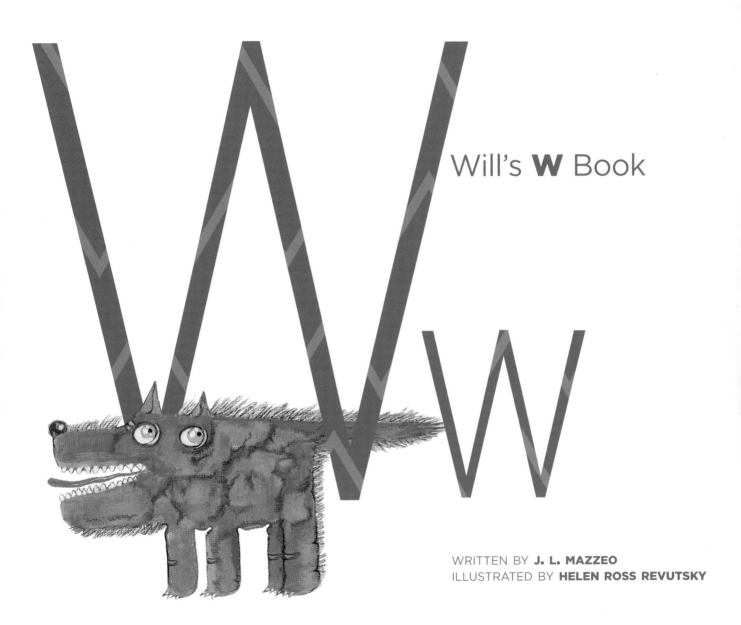

Will's **W** Book

WRITTEN BY **J. L. MAZZEO**
ILLUSTRATED BY **HELEN ROSS REVUTSKY**

dingles&company New Jersey

First Printing

Published By dingles&company
P.O. Box 508
Sea Girt, New Jersey 08750

LIBRARY OF CONGRESS CATALOG CARD NUMBER
2005932152

ISBN
ISBN-13: 978 1-59646-548-0
ISBN-10: 1-59646-548-4

Printed in the United States of America

My Letter Library series is based on the original concept of Judy Mazzeo Zocchi.

ART DIRECTION
Barbie Lambert & Rizco Design
DESIGN
Rizco Design
EDITED BY
Andrea Curley
PROJECT MANAGER
Lisa Aldorasi
EDUCATIONAL CONSULTANT
Maura Ruane McKenna
PRE-PRESS BY
Pixel Graphics

EXPLORE THE LETTERS OF THE ALPHABET WITH MY LETTER LIBRARY*

Aimee's **A** Book
Bebe's **B** Book
Cassie's **C** Book
Delia's **D** Book
Emma's **E** Book
Faye's **F** Book
George's **G** Book
Henry's **H** Book
Izzy's **I** Book
Jade's **J** Book
Kelsey's **K** Book
Logan's **L** Book
Mia's **M** Book
Nate's **N** Book
Owen's **O** Book
Peter's **P** Book
Quinn's **Q** Book
Rosie's **R** Book
Sofie's **S** Book
Tad's **T** Book
Uri's **U** Book
Vera's **V** Book
Will's **W** Book
Xavia's **X** Book
Yola's **Y** Book
Zach's **Z** Book

* All titles also available in bilingual English/Spanish versions.

WEBSITE
www.dingles.com
E-MAIL
info@dingles.com

My **Letter** Library

Ww

My Letter Library leads young children through the alphabet one letter at a time. By focusing on an individual letter in each book, the series allows youngsters to identify and absorb the concept of each letter thoroughly before being introduced to the next. In addition, it invites them to look around and discover where objects beginning with the specific letter appear in their own world.

Ww

A a B b C c D d E e F f G g

H h I i J j K k L l M m N n

O o P p Q q R r S s T t U u

V v **W w** X x Y y Z z

W is for Will.

Will is a wacky wolf.

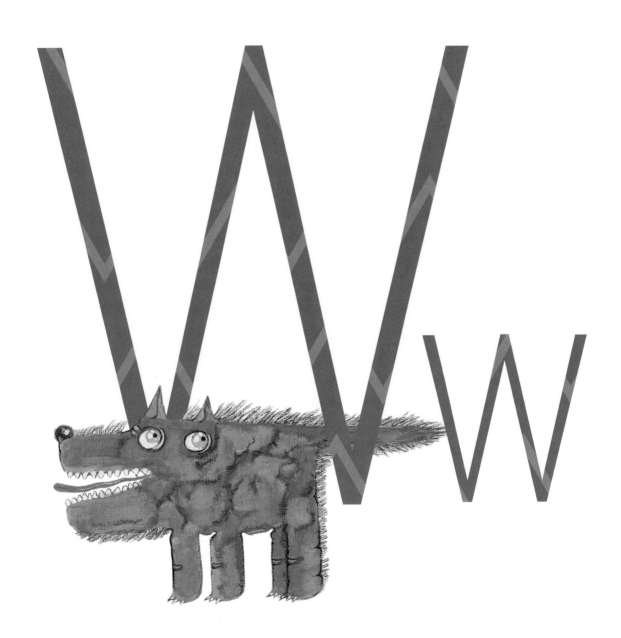

Hanging on

the wall in Will's room

are pictures of a **w**hale

holding its breath,

Ww

a **w**aterfall in Hawaii,

Ww

and a **w**oodpecker
waiting for a worm
it can eat.

W w

While visiting Will's room you will find a **w**easel,

Ww

a **w**asp looking for

an open window

to fly through,

Ww

and a **w**atch

that needs winding.

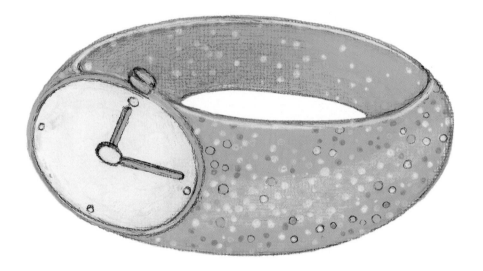

Ww

In Will's room

his friend Drake has

a **w**histle around his neck,

Ww

a **w**and

for doing magic tricks,

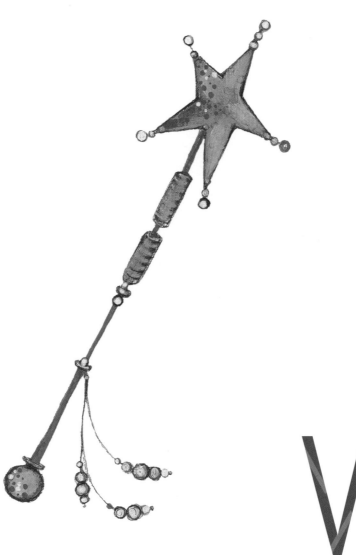

Ww

and a wedge of

watermelon for a snack.

W w

Things that begin with the letter **W** are all around.

PICTURE OF **W**HALE

PICTURE OF **W**ATERFALL

PICTURE OF **W**OODPECKER

WEASEL

WASP

WATCH

WHISTLE

WAND

WEDGE OF **W**ATERMELON

Where in Will's room
can they be found?

Have a **"W"** Day!

Read "W" stories all day long.
Read books about wolves, waterfalls, watermelons, and other **W** words. Then have the child pick out all of the words and pictures starting with the letter **W**.

Make a "W" Craft: A Whimsical Windsock
Cut the bottom off of a large cylinder-shaped oatmeal container.

Have the child decorate a piece of construction paper using crayons, markers, glitter, or whatever he or she chooses, then help the child put glue on the back and wrap it around the cylinder.

Help the child carefully cut a piece of tissue paper into six 1 1/2-inch-x-12-inch strips.

Now have the child glue one end of a tissue paper strip to the bottom of the cylinder and have him or her repeat this step with the remaining strips, going all the way around the cylinder.

Punch four holes in the top of the cylinder. Tie a 12-inch piece of string in each hole and join them at the top.

Hang the Whimsical Windsock outside and watch it wave in the wind.

Make a "W" Snack: Wonderful Waffle
- Toast a frozen waffle.
- Have the child choose a spread such as peanut butter, chocolate syrup, or jelly and spread it on the waffle.
- Then have him or her put a dollop of whipped cream on top of the spread and top it with bit-sized pieces of fresh fruits.
- Enjoy the Wonderful Waffle!

For additional **"W"** Day ideas and a reading list, go to www.dingles.com.

About **Letters**

Use the My Letter Library series to teach a child to identify letters and recognize the sounds they make by hearing them used and repeated in each story.

Ask:
- What letter is this book about?
- Can you name all of the **W** pictures on each page?
- Which **W** picture is your favorite? Why?
- Can you find all of the words in this book that begin with the letter **W**?

ENVIRONMENT
Discuss objects that begin with the letter **W** in the child's immediate surroundings and environment.

Use these questions to further the conversation:
- Have you ever seen worms in your yard?
- Do you have a watch? Can you tell time?
- Do you have a favorite food that begins with the letter **W**? If so, what is it?

OBSERVATIONS
The My Letter Library series can be used to enhance the child's imagination. Encourage the child to look around and tell you what he or she sees.

Ask:
- Have you every made a wish? If so, what did you wish for?
- Did you ever see a waterfall? Was it real or in a picture?
- What is your favorite **W** object at home? Why?

TRY SOMETHING NEW...
The next time you eat a slice of watermelon, save some seeds and ask a parent to help you plant them. Space the seeds about 1 inch apart and water them. Then keep watering them once a week. You may only grow a vine, or you might grow a small watermelon!

J. L. MAZZEO grew up in Middletown, New Jersey, as part of a close-knit Italian American family. She currently resides in Monmouth County, New Jersey, and still remains close to family members in heart and home.

HELEN ROSS REVUTSKY was born in St. Petersburg, Russia, where she received a degree in stage artistry/design. She worked as the directing artist in Kiev's famous Governmental Puppet Theatre. Her first book, *I Can Read the Alphabet,* was published in Moscow in 1998. Helen now lives in London, where she has illustrated several children's books.